Introduction to

Sanatana Dharma

By

Sri Dharma Pravartaka Acharya

Introduction to

Sanatana Dharma

By

Sri Dharma Pravartaka Acharya

ISDS

Omaha, NE, USA

2021

International Sanatana Dharma Society

13917 P Street

Omaha, NE 68137

www.dharmacentral.com

Other Works by Sri Dharma Pravartaka Acharya

Sanatana Dharma: The Eternal Natural Way

The Sanatana Dharma Study Guide

The Dharma Manifesto

The Vedic Way of Knowing God

Living Dharma: The Teachings of Sri Dharma Pravartaka Acharya

Radical Universalism: Are All Religions the Same?

Taking Refuge in Dharma: The Initiation Guidebook

The Shakti Principle: Encountering the Feminine Power of God

Introduction to Sanatana Dharma

Principles of Perfect Leadership

Lord of the Rings, Dharma and Modernity

The Vedic Encyclopedia

Narada Bhakti Sutras: Translation and Commentary

Vedanta: The Culmination of Wisdom

The Dharma of Wellbeing

Jnana Yoga: The Art of Wisdom

The Dharma Dialogues

Isha Upanishad: Translation and Commentary

Audio

Mantra Meditations (CD)

All these works can be purchased at:

www.dharmacentral.com

Table of Contents

Dedication

The present work is dedicated to Sri Narain Kataria, one of the nation's most fearless and tireless Vedic activist leaders, and my personal friend. He left us too soon. He is greatly missed.

x

Introduction

Over the last several decades, I have had the honor of giving thousands of talks on Vedic spirituality to diverse types of audiences. I remember one of the first times that I had delivered a spiritual talk to an audience made up specifically of Hindu youth. It was around 1995 in the Chicago area. I began my talk to a packed audience of young Indian Hindus ranging in age from 14-24 by asking them a rhetorical question.

"Of all the major world religions on the global stage today", I asked my audience, "which religious tradition is the most relevant and the most important one in our current age?" I waited patiently as the young faces in the audience all withdrew in intense thought. Each person – I was sure – was weighing the various merits and strengths of all the many world religions with which they were most familiar.

"Christianity!", suddenly cried out one young Hindu. "Islam…definitely Islam!", confidently proclaimed another. "I know. It's a trick question. Buddhism!" I waited patiently as answer after answer was given. While I was dismayed by the various wrong answers given to me by these young Hindus, I was also not really at all surprised.

When it seemed that there were finally no more volunteers to answer my rhetorical question, I then gave everyone the correct answer. "The most relevant and the most important religious tradition upon the entire earth today is Sanatana Dharma, what you may more commonly known by the term 'Hinduism'".

After a short period of stunned silence, all of the Hindu youth began to look around at each other, seemingly beckoning for permission from their peers to express some modicum of pride in their very own religious heritage. They all then looked at me with smiles of relief on their faces, many of them timidly nodding in agreement. Though they did not verbally state it, I could tell that the question that each one of these Hindu youth was now asking themselves within their own minds was "Why didn't I think of that!" Why, indeed, did they not?

Throughout the many decades that I have been closely working with the leaders of the Hindu community in America and globally, the level of concern about the spiritual state and the level of commitment of Hindu youth has been ever-present on the perplexed minds of Hindu leaders, *gurus* and parents. Repeatedly, I have been queried by such Hindu elders about what can be done to ensure that the younger generation of Hindus fully embraces their spiritual heritage with the pride, commitment and joy necessary to ensure the continuance of our tradition into the future.

There has been a severe disconnect between young Hindus and their ancient religious tradition for at least several decades now. There are two primary reasons why young Hindus have not shown quite the same amount of enthusiasm for their religion when compared to the youth of other religions. The first reason is a severe lack of authoritative and factual knowledge about Hinduism. There simply are very few Hindu leaders equipped with the legitimate knowledge and personal authority necessary to give these youth correct information. The second reason is a lack of personal spiritual practice (*sadhana*) and transformational experience on the part of most Hindu youth or members of their families. Hindu youth simply know very few people who actually practice the *sadhana* techniques of Vedic spirituality on a daily basis. As a consequence, they themselves do not practice or experience the states of transcendent bliss necessary to make Sanatana Dharma a living reality for them. It is impossible to practice any religion if there is a lack of knowledge about what the religion actually teaches, and if there is no encouragement to actually practice and experience the religion as a living tradition.

Introduction to Sanatana Dharma is a book that is designed to help its readers to fully understand the Vedic path in both of these crucial ways. This book was written to help people to both understand the Vedic tradition in an authoritative and factual way, as well as to explain how to actually practice, and thus experience, the primary elements of our Yogic tradition in a living and vividly meaningful way. Thus, while the primary audience of this book is the Hindu youth of the world, it is a book that can be beneficial to people of all ages and backgrounds in their quest to more fully understand the Vedic religion.

How the idea for this book came about is itself significant. Three weeks before he passed away, I had a meeting with my dear friend, the legendary Hindu activist Sri Narain Kataria, and several other Hindu leaders in New York. It was during this meeting that took place at the famous Ganesha temple in Flushing, Queens that the late Mr. Kataria asked me to write a special book that would serve the purpose of educating Hindu youth about their spiritual heritage, and that would set a fire of passion in them to practice their path with enthusiasm. Not knowing that this would be the very last time that I would have the opportunity to see one of my mentors and friends of the last 20 years, I agreed to take up Mr. Katariaji's request to create such a book. This book is the result of my undertaking.

This book is now humbly dedicated to the memory of Sri Narain Kataria, one of the greatest Hindu leaders and activists in American history. It pains me that he did not live long enough to actually see the book's publication. But I take solace in the fact that he is looking down from the heavens upon this work with approval.

In addition, I want to offer my special thanks Sri Arish Sahaniji for his tremendous support in the creation of this book. This book would not have been written without Mr. Sahaniji's wonderful encouragement.

I offer my sincerest and most profound thanks to Nick Kubash for the masterful creation of the beautiful cover art of this book. His portfolio can be found at: www.artstation.com/nickkubash.

My thanks are also given to Srimati Tulasi Devi Mandaleshvari for her brilliant creativity and aesthetic expertise in the formatting and editing of this book.

Finally, I want to offer my thanks to my disciple Jayadeva, who is responsible for arranging my very last meeting with Sri Narain Kataria in New York in 2015.

Aum Tat Sat

Sri Dharma Pravartaka Acharya
International Sanatana Dharma Society
March, 2021

Chapter 1:

The Great Awakening of Authenticity

There is a great awakening that is currently taking place among a vast number of sincere and intelligent people throughout our world the likes of which has not occurred for centuries. This great awaking is especially seen in the form of a new and rapid reembracing of spiritual authenticity - and a subsequent, thorough rejection of inauthentic forms of consumer-driven "spirituality". Multiple millions of people at present are searching for a true and authentic expression of spirituality that will provide them with the personal peace, life-meaning, real philosophical answers, and trusted guidance that their hearts have been so deeply yearning for in our current age of uninspiring materialism. People are now rejecting all forms of fake spirituality: from religious fanaticism and fundamentalism, to the vapid and infantile immaturity of New Age scam artists, to all forms of commercially-driven pop spirituality. Millions are now eagerly re-embracing the most authentic, ancient and time-tested form of traditional spirituality available in our world today. The world is now embracing Sanatana Dharma – the Eternal Natural Way.

Welcome to Sanatana Dharma

The Vedic tradition, also known as the religion of Sanatana Dharma, is the path that has been welcoming many of these sincere spiritual seekers in the last decade. Sanatana Dharma has been providing many millions of these earnest searchers for truth with the spiritual authenticity that they have been eagerly pursuing. The ancient spiritual tradition of Sanatana Dharma is at the very core of the great awakening of authenticity that is now occurring. And the foremost movement on earth that has been introducing many of these millions of people to the profound beauty of Vedic spirituality is the International Sanatana Dharma Society (ISDS). Founded in 1998, the International Santana Dharma Society has spearheaded the restoration of Dharma globally in many dozens of sectors and fields of human endeavor, including spirituality, philosophy, arts and culture, social, political, economic and academic areas.

The many tens of thousands of members, volunteers and devotees of the International Sanatana Dharma Society warmly welcome you to explore this ancient spiritual path with us as deeply as your heart desires, and to finally fully experience the personal peace, philosophical answers, deep meaning and spiritual joy that you have been seeking for all of your life. If living such a life is what you have been eagerly looking for, you are very welcome to become a Dharmi (a follower of Sanatana Dharma) and to join our loving family of Sanatana Dharma!

What is Sanatana Dharma?

Sanatana Dharma (translated as "the Eternal Natural Way") is many things. It is a spiritual path, a culture, a community, a world-view, a philosophical system, a way of being, and a total civilization. But, more than anything else, Sanatana Dharma is the most unique and personally rewarding religious tradition in the world. Sanatana Dharma, also often referred to as the Vedic tradition, has so much of value to offer us, both spiritually and practically. Of all the many benefits of Vedic spirituality, though, its greatest gift is that it gives our personal lives profound and very real spiritual meaning, along with the peace, joy and fulfillment that result from such meaning that is rooted in the Transcendent. Sanatana Dharma is God's divine gift to us, His beloved children.

As human beings, we have been gifted by God with a unique power that no other species on our planet has. We have the ability to question the ultimate meaning of our own existence. We have the intellectual means to ask about such topics as the existence and nature of God; the meaning of the cosmos that we are living in; the deepest essence of our own inner selves; our inevitable journey beyond the realm of death; and what is the practical path and course of behavior that we should follow in order to most maximally access our fullest spiritual potential.

Being presently in the human form of life, we are born to ask such important questions, and to seek the real answers to these inquiries. It is only in pursuing such questions, in fact, that we are fully manifesting ourselves as human persons. To not have the desire to ask such questions is to live the existence of a non-reasoning being. If you are reading this now, your desire is not to live as a non-thinking automaton, but to utilize your intellect toward knowing the important things in life. It is precisely our innate capacity for sincere philosophical inquiry that Sanatana Dharma exists to serve and to satisfy.

Ancient Wisdom for the Modern Era

Despite the revolutionary growth of communications and information technology in recent decades, the 21st Century has become an era in which a growing sense of confusion, disconnectedness, depression and a lack of meaning in our lives have become the norm within an increasing number of societies. Our smartphones, many have argued, have made us anything but smarter. If anything, the explosion of access to information has only led to most people now drowning in an over-abundance of worthless and unsatisfying information and degenerate entertainment.

Much of this useless information and entertainment has been purposefully designed by malevolent media manipulators, whose aim is to distract us with vapid entertainment, rather than enlighten us with truth. The result of this information implosion has been to only make the search for life's meaning even harder to ascertain in the midst of such a seemingly infinite cacophony of diverse, dishonest, distracting and unknowledgeable voices.

For those among us who are truly wise, however, it is understood that the search for answers to the most important questions of life is not to be pursued on the Internet, in the mainstream media, or through a phone app. Rather, the search for the Eternal can only be satisfied by humbly and patiently examining that specific literature, culture, set of spiritual practices and tradition that is itself eternal in its essence. Truth is eternal. Truth is revealed through the natural order. It is in embracing a path that is eternal, natural and perfect, and has therefore proven itself to be reliable, that we will begin to grasp the Eternal.

That ageless spiritual tradition that can deliver the Eternal Truth to us has been known in the ancient Sanskrit language for time immemorial by the term "Sanatana Dharma", or the Eternal Natural Way. Sanatana Dharma is not only humanity's greatest living spiritual heritage; it is the fulfillment of our deepest yearning to know Truth in the here and now. It is in Sanatana Dharma that we can find the authentic answers to life's greatest mysteries that we have so sincerely sought. Sanatana Dharma is not only the most ancient religious path on Earth, but it is also a vital, ever-fresh, and vigorously living way of being that is completely relevant to our lives today.

This is the case because, unlike any other spiritual tradition upon the Earth today, Sanatana Dharma is ably equipped to provide us with answers and a way of life that are not the result of human speculation, sectarian opinion, or commercially concocted and market driven pop spirituality. Rather, Sanatana Dharma represents the very essence of the Cosmos itself, and not just another empty dogma.

When we purchase an intricate piece of equipment or technology, there is always an owner's manual that comes along with the equipment to explain how to operate it in a safe, efficient and proper manner. It is the owner's manual that fully unlocks the equipment's full operating potential to its owner. In the same way, Sanatana Dharma is the self-generated owner's manual that the Cosmos itself provides us to understand and properly utilize its many confusing features. Without such an authorized manual, the universe will remain a consistently confusing, and at times even dangerous, home for us. It is for this reason that our spiritual tradition is named Sanatana Dharma, or the Eternal Natural Way. Sanatana Dharma is the eternal way by which nature herself reveals to us the true meaning of the world around us.

Sanatana Dharma is non-different from the essential being of the Cosmos itself. Dharma constitutes the subtle and flawless essence of the material world around us. As a result, the answers that Vedic spirituality offers us are better and more authoritative than any other spiritual tradition, philosophy, worldview or ideology that the world can provide us. Sanatana Dharma is not a dogma, but is based upon reason, logic, philosophy, and the intuitive insight of the successful sages of the past who derived their knowledge of the Cosmos from having spiritually intuited the silent voice of the Cosmos itself. It is the priceless heritage of these ancient sages that has been gifted to us to this very day in the form of Sanatana Dharma.

Dharma, Not Dogma

Being based upon pure spiritual and philosophical insight, rather than any form of blind faith or dogma, Sanatana Dharma is naturally the most reasonably tolerant, peaceful, and non-fanatical religion in the world today. Unlike any of the much more recent, sectarian religions that now inhabit our world,[1] Sanatana Dharma is not based on blind belief, deluded superstition, closed-mindedness, sectarian hatred, or fanaticism.

---

[1] Such as the Abrahamic ideologies, consisting of Judaism, Christianity, Islam and Marxism.

Rather, it is based upon a) the supportive guidance of the Vedic scriptures (the most ancient collection of writings ever recorded in human history), b) the living example of hundreds of generations of liberated *yogis*, sages and saints who traversed the path before us, including contemporary spiritual masters (*gurus*), c) your own free inquiry and intelligent discernment in searching for Truth, d) your personal and direct experience of God garnered through the disciplined practice of meditation, and e) respect for you as a free person and an intelligent seeker. Unlike many other religions, Sanatana Dharma is not here to merely dictate to you what you are to believe; but to help you come to your own reasonable conclusions through your own personal encounter with the Divine.

Dharma Transcends Time and Founder

Sanatana Dharma is the most ancient continuously practiced religion in the world. There is no religious tradition that is more ancient. Indeed, Dharma transcends all time. It is eternal. While all of the other major world religions can be traced back to an historical time of origin, Sanatana Dharma has no recognized beginning in human history.[2] Even more, there is no one person or collection of multiple persons who can be claimed as the "founder" of the Vedic tradition. The origination point of this tradition is to be found in the transcendent and eternally situated, spiritual realm (Vaikuntha) itself. This is another unique feature of the Vedic tradition that holds it apart from each and every other religion on the earth. Our Dharma is Sanatana; it is eternal!

As a result of its antiquity, its non-reliance on human founders, the profound knowledge that it reveals, and its eternal nature, the Vedic tradition was always deeply respected by many of the greatest minds throughout the history of both Europe and Asia. Many thousands of famous and illustrious people, ranging from Plato, Plotinus and Gautama Buddha in

---

[2] This fact is recognized both within the tradition itself, as well as by almost every credible scholar and professor of religious studies in the world.

the ancient world, to such modern figures as Ralph Waldo Emerson, Henry David Thoreau, Aldous Huxley, George Harrison - even Julia Roberts! - have all enthusiastically praised various aspects of Vedic spirituality.

Due to the spiritual peace, personal empowerment, as well as the healthy and satisfying lifestyle that it offers its followers, Sanatana Dharma has survived intact for over 5000 years in traceable historical terms, and for innumerable millennia before even then. It has survived the long course of history, when many other religions did not, because its teachings are time honored and true. In the same manner, Sanatana Dharma will never cease to be in the future. It will outlive every rival ideology on Earth precisely because it is non-different from the very Cosmos itself. Dharma is eternal.

Chapter 2:
The Scriptures of Sanatana Dharma

Somewhat similar to all of the other major world religions, Sanatana Dharma bases all of its teachings upon a specific set of scriptures that are accepted as being theologically authoritative. The scriptures of Sanatana Dharma are known as the Vedic scriptures. The Vedic scriptures constitute the highest and most reliable authority and source of accurate knowledge in our tradition.

The term "*Veda*" itself is translated into English as "knowledge" or "wisdom". The *Vedas* contain an extremely wide array of fields of knowledge: everything from overtly spiritual, religious and philosophical information, to even many secular fields and topics. Some of the more everyday topics revealed in the *Vedas* include architecture and city planning, arts and culture, politics, science, economics, martial arts and sciences, health and medicine, cosmology and history, among many hundreds of other fields. In this way, the ancient Vedic literature offers humanity a vast library of knowledge perfectly designed to understand and operate our world expertly on every level and in every domain of human concern.

The Vedic scriptures deliver knowledge that is revealed to a maximal degree of perfection. This is the case because, unlike the great majority of other literature in our world, the Vedic literature is not a set of books that originated in any way from the imperfect minds of flawed and limited human beings. Rather, the knowledge contained within the *Vedas* reveals the transcendental record of Truth that exists eternally in the form of a current of divine sonic vibration.

grant claims!

This eternal stream of perfect knowledge can only be accessed by perfected *yogis* and sages who have the yogic ability to transform themselves into transparent conduits of Truth. Like Dharma, *Veda* is an eternal phenomenon that can only be directly accessed by spiritually perfected beings. It is these perfected beings, known as *rishis*, who have the ability to chronicle this eternal Truth in the form of literature. Thus, the *Veda* is what is termed in Sanskrit *apaurusheya*, or "not man-made". No human hands or minds were involved in the origin of *Veda*. The *Veda* is, thus, perfectly divine in its foundational origin.

Questionable?

If there is any theological or philosophical claim that cannot be supported by an appeal to the authority of the Vedic scriptures, then that claim is understood by all sincere followers of Sanatana Dharma to be invalid and untrue. The Vedic scriptures represent the ultimate source and final arbiter of all truth claims.

Definition of a Dharmi

What constitutes a follower of Sanatana Dharma (a Dharmi) is not merely one's ethnicity, nationality, or any other material factor. The primary determinate

for whether a person is or is not a follower of
Sanatana Dharma is whether or not that person fully
accepts the Vedic scriptures as their ultimate guide in
life. If a person does not accept the perfect authority
and trusted guidance of the Vedic scriptures, then he
is by definition not a follower of Sanatana Dharma. If
a person does accept the Vedic scriptures as their
spiritual guide in life, then they are a Dharmi, a
follower of Sanatana Dharma.

The Vastness of the Vedic Library

Unlike the scriptures of the Abrahamic religions, the
Vedic scriptures do not consist of either just one
book, or even a small collection of texts. Rather, the
Vedic literature is a very large collection of sacred
books. Some of the better known texts include such
works as the *Bhagavad Gita*, the *Mahabharata*, the
Ramayana, the *Yoga Sutras*, and the 108 books known
as the *Upanishads*. There are many hundreds of such
individual texts that comprise the Vedic scriptures;
and all of these individual books are classified into

one or another genre, or class, of sacred literature. All genres of Vedic scriptures fall, first of all, under the two broad categories of either *shruti* ("What is Heard") or *smriti* ("What is Remembered"). The following chart illustrates a few of the major genres of Vedic scripture.[3]

---

[3] Again, these are all broad genres of literature. Within each specific genre, there are multiple texts. For example, there are 4 *Samhitas*, 108 *Upanishads*, 36 *Puranas*, 2 *Itihasas*, etc.

The Vedic Canon

Shruti	_Smriti_
Samhitas (Vedas)	_Puranas_
Brahmanas	_Sutras_
Aranyakas	_Pancharatras_
Upanishads	_Agamas_
Vedangas	_Tantras_
Upavedas	_Dharma Shastras_
	Itihasas (Two Epics)
	1. _Ramayana_
	2. _Mahabharata_
	2(a) _Bhagavad Gita_

The Vedic literature is truly massive in content. For a person who is just beginning their reading of the Vedic literature, I recommend that they start with the *Bhagavad Gita*. A good follow-up scripture to read after this is the *Srimad Bhagavatam*.

The philosophical teachings, practices and disciplines, as well as all of the ethical principles of Sanatana Dharma that have been practiced since the beginning of time, have all originated from the Vedic scriptures. Every teaching and practice that will be outlined in the next several chapters are all found in the *Vedas*.

Chapter 3:

The Philosophy of Sanatana Dharma

It is not possible to fully embrace a spiritual path unless that path has the ability to provide us with a completely satisfying philosophical explanation of our overall reality. Sanatana Dharma satisfies our philosophical inquiry perfectly. Sanatana Dharma has been renowned for thousands of years and by millions of spiritual seekers for having a thoroughly comprehensive, systematic and logically-supported philosophical world-view.

The philosophy of Sanatana Dharma offers us a complete accounting of the totality of human experience, including: why we exist; what is our true inner nature; what is God; what we are to practice in order to fully develop ourselves spiritually; and how we are to act toward others around us. Vedic philosophy covers every aspect of intellectual inquiry, from ontology and metaphysics, to epistemology,

ethics, aesthetics, politics, economics and cosmology.
Sanatana Dharma is not just a religion, but is a
comprehensive and thoroughly exhaustive philosophy
of everything!

According to Vedic philosophy, which is known in
the Sanskrit language as Vedanta (meaning the
Culmination of Wisdom), everything and anything in
reality that is either perceptual and/or conceptual can
be ultimately reduced to three different elemental
realities of being (ontologies). These three principle
realities are the following:

A) God (Sriman Narayana)

B) Individual Souls (Atman)

C) Materiality (Jagat)

Using these three categories of being as a starting
point, we will now briefly explore the philosophical

world-view of Sanatana Dharma,[4] starting with the most important of these three elemental realities: God.

A) God (Sriman Narayana)

For Sanatana Dharma, the Absolute reality is God. Having a deep belief in God, as well as devotion toward God, is central to what it means to be a follower of Sanatana Dharma. It is not possible to be simultaneously an atheist and a Dharmi. A person is either one or the other. Knowing God, experiencing God's living presence in one's life, and serving God with dedicated love and devotion is the meaning of life for all followers of Sanatana Dharma. But what, exactly, is God?

---

[4] For an extremely thorough and authoritative overview of Vedic philosophy, read *Sanatana Dharma: The Eternal Natural Way*, available at Dharmacentral.com.

More so than any other religious tradition on earth, the Vedic tradition reveals to us many important facts and details about the nature of God. There are, for example, many names of God that are found throughout the Vedic scriptures. Each of these names reveals a different attribute, aspect or title of God. Each one of these revealed and eternal names of God is sacred, and is seen as non-distinct from God Himself. Therefore, when we meditate upon a name of God, it is non-different from meditating upon God Himself. Of all the many names of God that are recorded in the Vedic scriptures, however, the most important and most intimately personal name of God is Sriman Narayana, which has the beautiful meaning of: The Auspicious Sustainer of All Beings.

Sriman Narayana (God) is the source and possessor of an infinite number of auspicious attributes, all expressed to a quantitatively infinite degree of qualitative perfection. God is of the nature of ultimate good, and does not possess anything contrary to good within His nature. In the same way that there can be no trace of shadow upon the surface of the Sun, evil cannot exist in the presence of God. Thus, God is the source of all that is good everywhere and anywhere. God is the source of, for example, all true love, wisdom, beauty, compassion, strength, fame, courage, eternality, discernment, detachment, and abundance, among an infinite number of other positive attributes and attainments.

Consequently, all positive attributes, states of being, experiences, and qualities that exist in this world that we experience as truly good, healthy and desirable ultimately have God as their source. Whereas God is the Infinite, we living beings also share in many of God's attributes, but to a finite and limited degree, and due only to having God as the very source of our own being.

God's essence is that of pure consciousness, or transcendent spirit. There is no trace of anything material in His nature. In His essential nature, therefore, God's being is thoroughly transcendent in relation to all of His creation. God is infinitely superior to physicality, to emotions, to the mind, the intellectual, or anything else that is not of the nature of His own pure consciousness. God is also infinitely superior to all other living beings, who all have God as their source and their sustainer. Nothing that is lessor than God can ever overtake, have control over, or be superior to God. He is situated supremely above and beyond both all living beings, as well as all insentient matter. This is because all sentient beings (Atman) and all insentient matter (Jagat) are His energetic by-products, and are thus thoroughly dependent upon Him for their very existence.

God never falls under illusion, ignorance, or mistaken perceptions or conceptions. God's knowledge and capacity to know are perfect always, and are unbounded. God never ceases to be God, or to even mistakenly forget – even momentarily - that He is God. Indeed, this is one of the many differing characteristics that are found between God and all other living beings. God never forgets His true nature; but we finite beings do possess the capacity to forget the nature of our true selves. This is why we are in illusion; whereas God is never in illusion.

God is beyond all materially perceptual and conceptual reality, as the very source and foundation of such material reality. This is because He is the source of all things. All of reality, both spiritual and material, including every living being, find their origin, their meaning, and their ultimate purpose in God.

B) Individual Souls (Atman)

To greater or lesser degrees, consciously or unconsciously, all human beings are seeking joy, fulfillment and Truth in our lives. We mistakenly seek such positive attainments in the external world due to our profoundly mistaken forgetfulness of the fact that such positive attainments are actually rooted in our own, internal spiritual nature. We seek truths and facts in the external world not realizing that God has already equipped us with inner wisdom. We seek beauty in the material world not realizing that our own souls have already been gifted by God with unimaginable beauty. We look for wealth in the world not realizing that our souls already possess the greatest of spiritual treasures. We fantasize about living in our material bodies forever, and never dying, forgetting that we are already eternal beings who never die. All the positive attainments that we have spent our entire lives looking for in the outer world already exists to complete perfection within our own God-gifted souls.

The only reason why we very often do not seem to consciously experience all of these desirable things within is due to the fact that most of us find ourselves in varying degrees of self-created illusion. We find ourselves in our current condition of illusion, dissatisfaction and suffering due to mistakenly identifying ourselves with objects, states of being, and desires that are not reflective of our true self. We identify with our fleeting ego, rather than with our true and eternal self. That true self, which is the very essence of our being, which is non-different from who we really are, is known in Sanskrit as *atman*, which is sometimes called "soul", "spirit", "true self", or "consciousness" in many modern languages.

The inherent nature of our soul (*atman*) is that our soul is eternal. It did not come into being when our present physical form was born; and it does not go out of being when our body eventually dies. Rather, there was never a time when our true self did not exist; nor shall it ever cease to be. Our soul transcends all materiality, all things that are temporary and imperfect. Our soul cannot be made wet by water or be made dry be wind. It cannot be cut, burnt, injured or stained. Though the body can be affected by either temporary pain or pleasure, and the many other dualities of this world, our soul is never affected by any of the temporary states of this material realm. Our soul transcends even the illusory experience of death.

While most of the Abrahamic religions teach that we possess a soul. Sanatana Dharma does not teach that we have a soul, in the same way that we have a liver, or a kidney, or a spleen. Our soul is not something that we have. Rather, it is something that we are. we are the soul. We are consciousness. We are *atman*.

The Origin of the Soul

Each and every soul (*atman*) in the material world was originally situated in the spiritual realm long before our present existence here. Every individual soul is a spark of consciousness that was originally situated in the unlimited, transcendental effulgence of God. We were an individual, conscious spark of God's unlimited light. To give a simple illustration of our pre-illusion status in the spiritual realm: God is compared to the Sun; while each individual soul was like the individual atoms of light that are situated in the effulgent rays of the Sun. Like the Sun, God is our source; and we were sustained within the rays of God's effulgent energy.

At a certain point in our personal development of awareness within that spiritual effulgence of God, each individual soul was eventually faced with a free-will choice. That choice was the decision to either a) continue exploring our true selves in loving relationship with God, or b) choosing to create an artificial self and exploring our false ego within the material aspect of God's power.

Those souls who chose to create an artificial sense of self and to reject God, now find themselves in a self-imposed state of illusion due to giving in to that false identity and false ego, and are thus now situated in the material world. The ultimate spiritual purpose of each of us is to eventually attain liberation from our self-chosen illusion, to transcend our suffering in the material world, and to again reenter into the spiritual realm to reclaim our path toward an eternal relationship with God in His highest spiritual domain, known as Vaikuntha, or the Kingdom of God.

Reincarnation, Karma and Liberation

Sanatana Dharma teaches us that we are not just our physical bodies. Rather, our eternal souls temporarily inhabit our material bodies for the purpose of living our lives in the material world. In the same way that a person puts on new clothes when the old clothes become old and torn, in a similar way, the soul acquires a new body upon the death of the old and worn-out physical form. Thus, the soul upon death transmigrates (reincarnates) to a new physical vehicle that is determined in accordance with his personal *karma* (previous ethical or unethical actions) and free will decisions.

While experiencing life in this material world, we find ourselves undergoing a self-imposed trajectory of repeated births and deaths as we traverse the various cycles of reincarnation that we have created for ourselves. With each human cycle of reincarnation, we are faced with the choice to either a) elevate ourselves spiritually, or b) to remain static in our spiritual progress, or c) to denigrate ourselves even further. If we choose to elevate ourselves, then our next birth will be in an advanced form of body/mind that is even more conducive for greater spiritual progress. But if we choose to denigrate ourselves by making bad moral decisions, then we will have to take birth in a lower form of life, in which our lower body will be reflective of our lowly behavior and mindset.

What determines whether we will have positive or negative life experiences from lifetime to lifetime are the free-will moral decisions that we make. We, and we alone, determine whether we will advance or regress spiritually. For every ethical or unethical decision that we choose to make, there will be an equal and opposite reaction in the future that will determine what type of life we will have in our subsequent future. If we do good, we will have good happen to us in the future. If we do evil, then we will have bad things happen to us in the future. This law of the universe is known as the principle of *karma*, and is designed to ensure that justice is always maintained and balanced in our cosmos. Thus, *karma* is a principle that celebrates our free-will choices, and that gives us the power to determine our own future – either for good or bad. *Karma* is a principle of freedom.

The Vedic tradition teaches us that the meaning of life for each of us as individual *atmans* is to achieve eventual freedom from this recurring cycle of birth and death. Our goal is to attain spiritual liberation, or enlightenment, and to reunite with God in eternal devotional relationship. It is for the sake of achieving this ultimate goal of liberation alone that we find ourselves in this world of material duality. Liberation, in turn, consists of two very closely aligned and sequential goals:

First, to fully know, realize and experience our true, eternal atman. This first goal is known as Self-Realization (*atma-jnana*). Self-realization must come first since we must first know the knower before we can know anything else.

2) The second goal of liberation is to fully experience the presence of God in our lives, and to serve God eternally in a state of loving, devotional awareness (*bhakti*). This second goal is known as God-Consciousness (*Brahma-vidya*). It is upon achieving these two goals that we can experience the highest degree of spiritual freedom, and thus achieve the greatest purpose of human life.

C) The Material World (Jagat)

Each one of us is an eternal soul who currently finds himself living in a material body. More, that material body finds itself in a world that is inherently designed as a place that is temporal, ever-changing, riddled with imperfections, and full of various sets of dualities (most notably, the duality of suffering and pleasure). The characteristics of this material world are in every way the very mirror opposite of the characteristics that are found in spiritual reality.

The material is temporary and impermanent; the spiritual is eternal and permanent. The material is fragmental and composed of parts; the spiritual reality is of the nature of unity. The material is often chaotic and conflictual; the spiritual is inherently of the nature of harmony and balance. Living beings in the material world are often motivated by the base instinct for survival; spiritually liberated beings are motivated by love and compassion. Everything in the material world is limited; the realm of consciousness is boundless. Materiality and consciousness are ultimately incompatible. Thus, the material world is not our true home.

The material world, however, is not in itself to ever be viewed as being necessarily bad, negative or evil in any way whatsoever. On the contrary, materiality is one of the many powerful energies of God that exists ultimately in His service. That being the case, the material world is, in itself, neither a good, nor an evil place. Rather, it is a neutral tool that can be used by its illusioned inhabitants for either good or evil purposes. The material world is merely a neutral environment that has been lovingly provided to us by God in order for His temporarily illusioned children to learn and to grow spiritually. Ideally, within the material world, we learn our mistakes and grow in our spiritual successes. It is up to us whether we use this gift from God as a tool for spiritual growth, or further bondage.

The material world is a gift from God for those of His children who rejected Him for the sake of illusion. The world exists in order to help us to eventually reembrace God as our source and ultimate goal. The material world is a realm in which we have mistakenly chosen to fully exercise our false ego and artificial sense of identity, and to explore our own material desires. This state of illusion will continue for us until the time eventually comes when we finally choose to fulfil our life's true purpose of learning how to transcend the material world by fully acknowledging the ultimate source of this material world, which is God.

In this way, the material world around us can be compared to a very good school, in which we learn a multitude of life lessons – both negative and positive - from our many experiences here. The spiritual end-goal of our experiences in this material "school" is to finally "graduate" by achieving liberation (*moksha*) from the illusion and ignorance that we mistakenly chose.

It is upon achieving such liberation from our illusion that we can now fully understand the nature of the material world around us as not merely a place of suffering and hardships, but as a school-house that has been lovingly provided to us by the infinite grace of God. It is with this proper vision that materiality itself can now be used in God's service. This is because every positive thing in this material world can be transcendentalized by the spiritually motivated person in the direct service of God.

In this way, the sincere follower of Dharma approaches his life in the world in a very positive and joyful manner. He can live a life in which he balances his spiritual insight with his material needs in such a way that he rejects nothing that helps him to further his loving service toward God and toward all living beings. Sanatana Dharma is, thus, a life-affirming world-view that encourages us to live a life of spiritual balance and harmony even while still situated in the material world.

Chapter 4:

Sadhana: Practicing Sanatana Dharma

Of all the many reasons why you should consider being a Dharmi, the most important one is that it is through Sanatana Dharma that you can have a personal and vividly transformative experience of God's loving presence in your life. The ultimate goal of Sanatana Dharma is not merely to have a good theological understanding of God's nature, but to experience God's presence in a radically personal and vividly real way. When God is placed in the center of your personal life, and in the center of your family's life, there is no challenge, no problem, no illness, and no difficulty that you cannot face with courage and resilience. Sanatana Dharma is the most direct and practical path there is for knowing God's love and grace in your life.

The way that we gradually bring ourselves closer to achieving the cherished goals of self-realization and

God-consciousness is by practicing the methodical path of self-improvement that is laid out in the Vedic scriptures, under the direct guidance of a qualified *guru* (enlightened spiritual teacher). Such expertly guided, rigorous daily practice is known as *sadhana*.

Sadhana involves many different spiritual techniques and practices that deliver a steady course toward self-development, all of which are performed with great focus, discipline, resilience, patience and faith. Such practices include meditation, breath work (*pranayama*), *mantra* recitation, meditative ritual, prayer, the strict observance of ethical and moral precepts, as well as often observing vows of austerity and asceticism (*tapasya*) that lead to self-improvement.

Sadhana is practiced in a very systematic and methodical way that is akin to a sacred science of personal spiritual growth. *Sadhana* is designed to gradually, yet thoroughly, transform the active spiritual practitioner in ways that are both deeply experienced and all-encompassing in their range. In this chapter, we will look at only a small number of these highly empowering spiritual practices that all followers of Sanatana Dharma can choose to begin practicing in their daily lives.

Developing Healthy Faith

One of the most important personal virtues that a person must have in order to successfully practice *sadhana* is faith: Faith in God, faith in one's spiritual teacher (*guru*), faith in one's goal, faith in the path that one is following, and faith in oneself as a sincere spiritual seeker. Faith is arguably an important element of all religious traditions. For the Vedic tradition, however, the conscious practice of faith (*shraddha*) is never to be confused with the idea of blind faith that is found in many of the more recently created religious denominations. Rather, in Sanatana Dharma, faith is never blind or dogmatic. Faith is based upon the evidence one's direct personal experience, and not on any sort of blind or fanatical consent.

The Importance of Having a Guru

A very important practical foundation of Sanatana Dharma consists in seeking expert guidance from a qualified and authentic spiritual teacher, called a "*guru*" in Sanskrit. It is the authentic and experienced *guru* who has the ability to expertly guide us in our *sadhana* practice. To find such an authentic *guru* in the 21st century has become quite difficult compared to past eras. But it becomes easier once you know exactly what you are looking for.

An authentic *guru* is a person who has both in-depth scriptural and philosophical knowledge, as well as a vivid and very personal experiential realization of Truth. A *guru* teaches by his own personal example by exemplifying in his being the very essence of Dharma and Vedic teachings in his own life. As a result of his high degree of enlightenment and spiritual attainment, the *guru* is offered maximal respect, reverence and fidelity by sincere spiritual seekers.

If a person is truly genuine in his spiritual pursuit, and wishes to have legitimate and trusted guidance in his spiritual journey, then that person must ultimately find and learn from a qualified and authentic Vedic *guru*. Such an authentic *guru* is admittedly difficult to find in our current century. The members, students and disciples of the International Sanatana Dharma Society are very fortunate to have direct access to an exceedingly authentic lineage of such *gurus*. If you are sincerely ready to seek expert guidance in the practice of *sadhana*, contact the International Sanatana Dharma Society today by visiting Dharmacentral.com and become involved in our Vedic community. Also, read the book *Taking Refuge in Dharma: The ISDS Initiation Guidebook*, also available on Dharmacentral.com

Devotion and Surrender to God

Devotion (*bhakti*) and surrender to God (*prapatti*) constitute the two most important elements of all spiritual practice. For the sincere spiritual aspirant, every single aspect of *sadhana* must be grounded in devotional consciousness. Indeed, any form of "Yoga" practice in which devotional consciousness is not central to every aspect of the practice cannot be legitimately called authentic Yoga at all. Whether we are practicing meditation, Yoga, ritual, breathwork (*pranayama*) or any other systematic Vedic practice designed to help us grow in our spiritual development, devotion and surrender to God must always be present in the heart and mind of the spiritual practitioner. It is precisely the practice of devotional consciousness while performing one's *sadhana* that gives all spiritual purpose and empowerment to the *sadhana* itself.

Yoga: The Technology of Self-Realization

Actively practicing spirituality in our daily life is just as important, if not more so, than just understanding spirituality on the philosophical or intellectual level. The way that we progress spiritually is by doing, and not merely by thinking. We grow by following a disciplined daily regimen of practices that are designed to gradually refine our minds and hearts, to give us self-realization, and to eventually reveal the presence of God to us. The most important spiritual exercises (*sadhana*) of Sanatana Dharma consists of the practice of Yoga.

When we hear the term "Yoga" in the modern, industrialized world, we tend to think only of the physical poses (*asanas*) that have made Yoga so popular throughout the world. Yoga, however, consists of much more than only the very effective and healthy physical exercises that are associated with this path. Rather, practiced in its full form, Yoga is comprised of many integral practices that benefit every aspect of our being, and that are meant to bring us gradually to spiritual perfection. Yoga benefits us physically, emotionally, psychically, mentally, intellectually, and of course spiritually. These highly effective processes include very precise exercises that have the potential to fully maximize the power of our breath, concentration, detachment from false ego, mastery over our senses, keen focus, resilience, greater intellectual discernment, pure devotion toward God, as well as the achievement of physical health.

Yoga is non-different from the religion of Sanatana Dharma. Indeed, the practice of Yoga spirituality is nothing less than Sanatana Dharma in practical application. If a person is practicing Yoga, then they are – knowingly or not – practicing the religion of Sanatana Dharma. Finding a well-trained Yoga teacher today who teaches the fully authentic Yoga system that is firmly rooted in the Vedic tradition has become quite challenging. The International Sanatana Dharma Society teaches the Yoga system in its fully authentic and Vedic form. For genuine guidance in your Yoga practice, please feel free to visit Suryavedahealing.com. Suryaveda Healing is the very best resource on the Internet for information and guidance on the practice of Yoga, as well as Ayurvedic herbalism and natural health.

While Yoga helps us to maximize our full potential though many powerful and proven techniques, the very heart of all Yoga practice is to be found in the art of meditation.

Meditation: The Heart of All Sadhana

The one practice that is of central importance in the *sadhana* system of both Sanatana Dharma and the path of Yoga is meditation. Meditation is the most powerful and effective tool of self-transformation in existence. It is through the daily discipline of meditation that we achieve every important spiritual goal. But it takes a proper understanding of what meditation is, as well as expert guidance by a true and authentic *guru*, to practice meditation in a way that will yield meaningful results.

The Object of Meditation

The process of meditation consists of the purposeful, calm focus of one's attentive awareness upon on a single object. What the object actually is upon which we meditate is the most crucial element of meditation. We become like that object that we meditate upon. For this reason, we should not meditate on simply anything. Indeed, any supposed meditation teacher who claims that it does not matter what our object of meditation is has revealed himself or herself to be someone who actually knows nothing about meditation.

Rather, we should always strive to have God as the actual object and focal point of our meditation practice. This is the case because there is nothing in existence that is higher, greater or more suitable as the supreme object for meditation than God. The highest form of meditation that is recognized in both Sanatana Dharma and Yoga is, therefore, the practice of devotional meditation in which God is the focal point of meditation.

How to Meditate

While there are several legitimate forms of meditation upon God that are recognized in the Vedic tradition, the most prevalent and effective meditation practice is the method of meditating directly upon the divine names of God in the form of *mantras*, or divinely revealed sound vibrations. Of all the authentic *mantras* that are revealed in the Vedic scriptures, the most important is the *mantra*:

Aum Namo Nārāyanāya

(Sanskrit: ॐ नमो नारायणाय)

The translation of this *mantra* is "I offer my humble obeisances to that Absolute who is the sustainer of all beings." Serious members of the International Sanatana Dharma Society meditate upon this sacred *mantra* daily in order to gradually increase their personal realization of God's presence in their lives.

The actual process of meditation is quite easy. It involves the three stages of:

A) Breath Concentration

B) Mantra Recitation

C) Breath Concentration

Meditation Procedure: This is a brief explanation of how you can immediately begin to have a daily meditation practice in your life. An important first step is that a specific location in your home should be set aside for meditation. If possible, meditation should be done in this same dedicated area of your home each day. The area where you meditate should be clean, quiet, and without distractions.

You should have a sacred image (either a statue, or a poster, or a painting, etc.) of Krishna or Narayana placed in your meditation room on a clean table or shelf. Before you begin your meditation practice, first light a stick of incense and slowly, reverently, wave the stick of incense with great devotion in a clockwise circle several times toward the sacred image. Placing the stick of incense safely in an incense holder, you may now sit down either in a cross-legged position on the ground (preferably) or else in a chair facing the sacred image.

Sitting with your eyes closed, the initial stage of meditation is to first focus all of your awareness on your breath – the feeling of your breath as you inhale and exhale, the very sound of your breath if you can hear it. The goal of breath concentration is to consciously relax your body and mind as much as possible before beginning to recite the *mantra*. Removing any other thoughts, sensations or perceptions from your mind, focus solely on your breath. Perform this breath concentration for several minutes.

The second stage is now to begin to recite the *mantra* **Aum Namo Nārāyanāya** for approximately ten minutes,[5] focusing all your awareness and concentration on the vibration of the sound. When you are done meditating on the *mantra*, the final stage is to, again, silently focus your full awareness on your breath for several minutes. After this, your meditation session is now over and you may open your eyes and resume your day.

Meditation should be practiced every single day, without fail. It is consistency in your daily practice that leads to gradual spiritual advancement, and to achieving the eventual goal of spiritual liberation. If a day should come in which you did not have a chance to meditate, however, do not become discouraged by this, and simply resume your practice again the next day. Any progress that you have made on the path toward liberation is never lost. Rather, you always

---

[5] You can always recite the *mantra* for longer if you want to and if you are able. The goal is to try to gradually increase the duration of time that you recite the *mantra*.

resume again from wherever you left off. Such is the nature of God's grace upon His devotees.

Important Vedic Holy Days

Vedic culture is a rich, diverse and immeasurable tapestry of beautiful celebrations of the Transcendent. There are many dozens of holy days that are observed in the Vedic community. We use these days to deepen our spiritual understanding and experience as we contemplate the meaning of the day. Some of these holy days, however, are of much more importance than others.

The following is a list of the most important holy days that all followers of Sanatana Dharma should observe each year. Please note that the Vedic calendar (known as the Yugabda calendar) is based upon a lunar calculation, and not the solar calculation of the West. As a result, it is not possible to give exact days of each holy day, since these will vary from year to year. Consequently, the exact dates are only approximations. Check with your local Vedic calendar (this information is easily available online) for the exact dates within any specific year.

Rama Navami (early April): This is the appearance day of the *avatara* (incarnation) Sri Rama. Rama appeared upon the Earth to rule as a perfect Chaktravartin, or Dharma Ruler, thus showing the world what it means to personify Dharma both in one's self and in a nation's governance. Worship of Sri Rama is performed on this day, along with a daylong fast that is ended with a feast of sanctified food (*prasada*).

Guru Purnima (early July): On this day, the principle of Sri Guru is celebrated throughout the Vedic community. We offer our obeisances to our own *guru*, and to all legitimate *gurus*, on this day. In addition to offering respects to our spiritual masters, we offer our respects to all the teachers who have positively impacted our lives. Praise is offered to the *guru*, and donations are given to the *guru* on this day.

Sri Krishna Janmashtami (late August or early September): This is the appearance day of the *avatara* (incarnation) Sri Krishna. Devotees of Sri Krishna will fast on this day until midnight, finally breaking the fast at midnight with a feast of sanctified food (*prasada*). We will also engage in devotional songs and reading the sacred story of Krishna's appearance and activities all throughout the day. Worship of Sri Krishna is performed throughout this day as well. This is the most important and joyous of all the Vedic holy days.

Dipavali (mid-October or mid-November): This day is also known as the "Festival of Lights". It celebrates the return of Sri Sri Sita Rama to their capital city of Ayodhya after 14 years in exile. The Vedic scripture known as the *Ramayana* explains that when Sita and Rama were flying back to the city in Their *vimana* (flying vehicle), the residents of Ayodhya were so overjoyed that they lovingly lit up millions of small lamps throughout the city so that Sita and Rama could easily find Their way back to them. This holy day celebrates the victory of good over evil, and the triumph of the light of Truth over the darkness of ignorance. On this day, we light *dipas* (ghee-wick lamps) and place them both inside and outside the house in commemoration of the return of Sita and Rama to Ayodhya.

Celebrating these sacred days, in addition to many other spiritual, social and cultural activities, helps to solidify a strong sense of belonging among members of the Vedic community.

Vedic Community

This brings us to one of the most important aspects of practicing Sanatana Dharma that ensures our continued spiritual growth on this path. The practice of spirituality is something that can, and should, be experienced through a healthy balance of individual, personal spiritual work, coupled with spiritual growth that is encouraged in the association with other sincere and encouraging people who share our Vedic path.

Dealing with the latter, the idea of being part of a greater Vedic community has always been encouraged as a vital aspect of spiritual growth. We need the association of fellow devotees in order to further our spiritual advancement. It is in actively associating with other people on the Vedic path that we gain inspiration from others, give inspiration to others, as well as share insights and wisdom with each other.

When you become a follower of Sanatana Dharma, you are joining a family of over a billion fellow devotees of this ancient path. You become part of a global community in which you have brothers and sisters in Dharma who reside in almost every single nation in the world. The International Santana Dharma Society is on the very forefront of creating a strong sense of healthy and supportive community within contemporary Vedic society.

Becoming a member of the International Sanatana Dharma Society is the very best way that you can connect with the greater Vedic community. If you are ready to adopt Sanatana Dharma as your chosen religious path, consider joining the ISDS today. To become a member of the ISDS, please visit: Dharmacentral.com/membership.html. You are warmly welcome to begin your journey of Sanatana Dharma with us.

Chapter 5:

The Ethics of Sanatana Dharma

What it means to be a sincere and serious follower of Sanatana Dharma is that we strive with determination to be ethical and virtuous in every aspect of our lives. Living an ethical and virtuous life is considered to be so central to the practice of Sanatana Dharma that I have decided to have an entire chapter dedicated to this important topic.

Being a virtuous and noble person is indispensable for anyone who wishes to grow spiritually. Thus, leading an impeccably ethical and morally thoughtful lifestyle is central to the life of all serious Dharmis. In our modern era, in which some pseudo-intellectuals will pronounce ethics to be relative, subjective or even non-existent, it is more crucial now than ever before that serious spiritual practitioners not shy away from fully embracing a life of goodness, morality and ethical behavior. There are many helpful ethical guidelines that are provided throughout the Vedic scriptures that are designed to help transform us into highly virtuous people.

A few examples of the most important of these ethical guidelines are:

- Ethical vegetarianism
- The avoidance of violence
- Not lying
- Not stealing
- Strict monogamy and fidelity in marriage
- The avoidance of all intoxicants (specifically all drugs, alcohol and tobacco)
- Seeking excellence and nobility in all of our thoughts, speech and deeds

One famous listing of principles of virtue that all Dharmis strive to exemplify in their lives is called the Yamas and Niyamas. These ten principles are found within both the religion of Sanatana Dharma and the practical system of Yoga. These ten principle are as follows:

Yamas

    a) Non-violence

    b) Truthfulness

    c) Non-stealing

    d) Sexual restraint

    e) Non-attachment.

Niyamas

    a) Contentment

    b) Discipline/austerity

    c) Study of Vedic scriptures

    d) Devotion to God

    e) Cleanliness

It is in following such virtue principles that Dharmis consciously avoid those negative behaviors that will lead only to further illusion and bondage, and cultivate those positive behaviors that will further elevate us in every important aspect of our lives. These are only a small sampling of the many ethical guidelines that all sincere Dharmis follow, and do not exhaust the total number of ethical principles that are taught in Sanatana Dharma.[6] By following the moral guidelines of Sanatana Dharma, the Dharmi transforms himself into a person of virtue, and ensures his own systematic spiritual growth, as well as becomes a blessing to his entire community.

---

[6] For a much deeper discussion of the many ethical principles that Dharmis follow, read *Sanatana Dharma: The Eternal Natural Way*, which can be found at dharmacentral.com.

Chapter 6:
Sanatana Dharma, Not Hinduism

One of the most glaring misconceptions about our spiritual heritage that is in the process of being corrected is the very name of our tradition itself. The true name of our religion is in actuality not "Hinduism", and followers of our path are not "Hindus". The word "Hindu" is not a recognized Sanskrit term (the sacred language of our sacred Vedic scriptures), and is not found anywhere within the texts of the accepted Vedic scriptures (the *shrutis* and *smritis*). From where did the term "Hindu" arise, then, and how has it now become such a prevalent term for our religion in mainstream society?

It was persons who were situated outside of our tradition who originally forced the term "Hinduism" upon our tradition. It is understood by every scholar of religious studies, and by the vast majority of modern Vedic leaders, that the term "Hindu" first originated from a grammatical mistake that occurred in the Persian language.

It is a grammatical feature of the ancient Persian language that the letter 's' did not exist in ancient Persian. Thus, in the ancient Persian language, the letter 's' is automatically changed to the letter 'h' grammatically. Persians historically referred to the culture, religion and people who lived on the other side of the Sindhu River (that is, modern day India) as the Sindhus. The 's' grammatically being changed into an 'h', the so-called "Sindhus" became known to the Persians as "Hindhus". It was much later that the British who had subsequently colonized India then altered the word even further still by removing the second 'h'.[7] Thus, "Hindhu" became the modern word "Hindu".

---

[7] European languages do not contain aspirates such as 'dh', 'bh', etc.

As a result of this very convoluted origin of the word "Hindu", every time we refer to our religion as either "Hindu" or "Hinduism", we are actually using a corruption of a corruption of a word that had no actual spiritual meaning to begin with, and that was imposed upon our religion by people who did not follow our religion. It is for this reason that it is imperative for all followers of the Vedic tradition to reembrace the actual name of our religion, which is "Sanatana Dharma". Our religion is Sanatana Dharma; and followers of our religion are known as Dharmis.

Even the original word "Sindhu" that was used by the ancient Persians only designated nothing more than a limited geographical region of the South Asian subcontinent. It was a word that was severely limiting in its scope and vision. The term Sanatana Dharma in comparison to the word "Hinduism", on the other hand, is a beautiful and profound name that points to the eternal and deeply philosophical nature of our way of life. Our religion is not a place. It is not a subcontinent. It is an eternal way of being. Sanatana Dharma is not only the accurate name for our religion, it is also majestic and unlimited in its scope!

Rather than insulting our own religious tradition by using a name that was artificially imposed upon us by non-Vedic people, it is crucial that we once again embrace the name of our religion that the religion itself prefers to be known by. The name of our religion that is actually found in the scriptures (*Shastras*) of our religion is "Sanatana Dharma". But why is it so important for us to re-embrace the original and authentic name of our religion?

After a thousand years of horrific persecution at the hands of aggressive and totalitarian ideologies,[8] our religion finds itself today in the process of reclaiming its outstanding heritage. How can we, as a Vedic people, wholly embrace and thoroughly practice our

---

[8] Very specifically Islam and Christianity, then followed later in the 20th century by the ravages of secular Marxism.

spiritual path, with the pride and commitment necessary to ensure its survival, when we have not even been able to correctly refer to our own religion by its real name? By insisting that the name of our religion is "Hinduism", non-Vedic people have deprived us of the right and the power inherent in choosing our own identity. By reembracing the true name of our religion – Sanatana Dharma – we are finally wresting control of our identity away from those who would impose a false identity upon us, and placing the control of the terminology associated with the Vedic tradition squarely where it belongs: in the hands of the Vedic people and the Vedic tradition itself.

It has been for this reason that I personally began a lonely campaign almost thirty-five years ago to have our people begin to refer to our religion once again as Sanatana Dharma. I am happy to see that so many Vedic leaders and followers have now listened to my arguments and have begun to do exactly that. Now, thirty-five years after I began my solitary efforts, the term Sanatana Dharma has been embraced by multiple millions of our people. Now we can all say with a well-earned pride: "My religion is Sanatana Dharma. I am a Dharmi."

Unfortunately, even though it is the case that Sanatana Dharma is an eternal manifestation of Truth, and represents the most advanced spiritual civilization that the world has ever known, this fact alone has not prevented our tradition, in the form of modern "Hinduism", from being one of the least understood and most surreptitiously imitated religions in modern times.

Indeed, while there are certainly some misconceptions about many other religions, I have argued in the past that there are probably more misconceptions, stereotypes and outright lies about the Vedic path than there are about every other single religion on Earth combined! Many such basic misconceptions can be seen on the Internet, even on websites as massive and seemingly "authoritative" as Wikipedia (a

definitely not so!

terrible source of information on Sanatana Dharma).

Much of this widespread ignorance about the Vedic tradition is due to an innocent lack of knowledge. Some of it, however, is due to a systematic and deliberate attempt by atheist materialists and Marxist globalists to purposefully mislead the public about the true nature of our religion. Similarly, these misconceptions can be blamed on both outsiders to our religion who purposefully wish to denigrate our religion, as well as on many misinformed and misguided leaders and *"gurus"* from within our very religion itself who often naively repeat the lies of anti-Vedic assailants.

Among other positive goals, it is my hope that this book will help to dispel many of the misconceptions and stereotypes about Sanatana Dharma that have so undermined our religion to the point that even many very religious followers of our path today have come to believe in some of these misconceptions. In order to quickly dispel a number of these misconceptions, the next chapter will address several of the most prevalent of these misconceptions about the Vedic tradition.

Chapter 7:
Some Misconceptions

In the following section, I will provide a short list of some of the more outrageous notions that some people believe about the Vedic tradition, as well as explaining the factual information on these various topics.

1) "Dharmis are idol worshipers."

This assertion is completely false. Dharmis are not idol worshipers. Sanatana Dharma does, indeed, employ the use of sacred imagery (known as *murti*) in both worship and meditation practice, as do the vast majority of ancient religions throughout history. Such sacred imagery, however, are not "idols" in the strict and proper definition of this word, as used to denote the superstitious worship of made up visual fabrications. Rather, the sacred images employed in Sanatana Dharma are sanctified symbolic portals of reverential focus that are divinely revealed to exact specifications in the Vedic scriptures. Such sacred images are not considered to be literally God, but rather, they are used as sacralized focal points of meditation and contemplation. The use of such sacred imagery is not based upon superstition, but upon spiritual science! It is in meditating upon such sacred images that we incorporate into our own being the positive and purifying power of God.

2) "Dharmis are polytheistic."

Sanatana Dharma is not, and has never been, a polytheistic religion. The official theological position of the Vedic tradition concerning the nature of the Absolute is termed panentheistic[9] monotheism. This theological principle states that God is both fully transcendental to His creation, while also being imminently present in all of creation. Sanatana

---

[9] The term panentheism is never to be confused with the somewhat similar sounding word pantheism.

Dharma teaches that there is ultimately one supreme being, who is the absolute One (*ekam*), without rival, and who is unitary in His essential being. This one supreme God is the source and sustainer of all reality.[10]

In addition to the existence of the one supreme being, however, Sanatana Dharma reveals to us that there is also a myriad hierarchy of powerful benevolent beings who are vastly superior to human beings, but who are also all subservient to God. These powerful and benevolent beings are called *devas* (lessor gods) and *devis* (lessor goddesses). These beings are roughly similar to the concept of angels as understood in the Western world.

---

[10] Some of these same concepts can be seen in the historically later religion of Christianity. I have argued that much of Christian theology concerning the nature of God was borrowed, both directly and indirectly, from the much more ancient religion of Sanatana Dharma.

The *devas* and *devis* are all servants of God, as are potentially all human beings as well. While such beneficent beings are quite powerful, however, they are never to be confused as being the same as God. So, Sanatana Dharma is not polytheistic in the strict sense of believing that the Absolute consists of a committee or pantheon of individual gods. Rather, we are panentheistic monotheists, we believe that there is one supreme and transcendent God who blesses all of reality with His divine presence.

3) "Vedic spirituality is purely 'magical thinking' and irrational; it is not philosophical or rational."

This is another ill-informed stereotype about the Vedic path that has gained widespread prominence - especially in the post 1960s era – but which actually has no basis in fact whatsoever. There is nothing irrational, New Age, or magical in Vedic thought or practice. Serious practitioners of Sanatana Dharma do not engage in any form of "magical thinking" at all.

Sanatana Dharma is a path that stresses the full development of both a) experiential spiritual unfoldment, closely coupled together with b) a deep philosophical/intellectual understanding. Neither the experiential, nor the philosophical, aspects of our search for Truth should detract from the other. Rather, a serious follower of the Vedic way uses both direct spiritual experience and philosophical discernment together in spiritual growth. While it is true that the foremost concern for spiritual practitioners in Sanatana Dharma is to ultimately experience the presence of God in a vivid and ecstatic yogic way, the Vedic tradition teaches us that the journey to God can be neither irrational, nor anti-intellectual. We reject the irrational.

On the contrary, Sanatana Dharma is a tradition that has always laid a tremendous amount of importance upon the use of philosophy, reason, logic and discernment in the search for, and the acquisition of, truth. Some of the world's greatest philosophers and scholars in such fields as ethics, metaphysics, epistemology, ontology, aesthetic theory, political science, economics, science and cosmology are to be found throughout the history of the Vedic tradition. Some of these incomparable philosophers include: Vyasa, Patanjali, Yajnavalkya, Ramanuja, Vijnanabhikshu, Jiva Gosvami, etc. Sanatana Dharma does not in any manner reject the use of philosophy and intellectual means in the pursuit of Truth.

4) "Sanatana Dharma is the religion of India".

One of the most pervasive and pernicious myths about Sanatana Dharma is that our religious tradition is non-different from the present nation-state of India, and that one can only be a follower of Sanatana Dharma if he is of Indian ancestry. Nothing could be further from the truth.

Not all Sanatana Dharmis are Indian, and not all Indians are Sanatana Dharmis. While it is true that in very recent centuries, the modern nation of India represents the nation with the largest population of Dharmis in the world, in actuality followers of Sanatana Dharma can be found in almost every nation and among almost every ethnicity on earth. There are followers of Sanatana Dharma who can be found among a very wide number of ethnic groups and nationalities throughout the world, including across the entire continent of Europe, all of South-East Asia, East Asia, the Americas, and many other regions.

Indeed, at one point in history, over 2500 years ago, the Vedic tradition represented the largest geographic expanse of any religion in history! Around the time of the Buddha (circa 6th century BC) the Vedic civilization had a geographical vastness that included roughly two-thirds of Asia, stretching from Persia (present day Iran), Central Asia, and much of the Middle-East, all the way to the Philippines, and including everything in between those two geographic points. I and many other Vedic leaders have argued that Sanatana Dharma was also the original religion of all of Europe previous to the coming of Judaism and Christianity to that continent. Sanatana Dharma was, at one time in history, the primary religion of the vast majority of the world.

Sanatana Dharma is not an Indian religion. It is not an Asian religion. It is not a South-Asian religion. It is not an Eastern religion. Sanatana Dharma is an eternal and universal religion.

One does not have to be of specifically Indian nationality at all, or even have any interest in India, or in Indian culture or history, in any way in order to follow Sanatana Dharma. One simply has to have a deep and sincere desire to know Truth. India and Vedic culture are not synonymous in any way.

5) "The Vedic tradition teaches people to be passive and weak."

This is not at all true. Unknown to most people, Sanatana Dharma has always been a spiritual tradition that is very much steeped in a very strong warrior ethos and culture. Some of the most important spiritual figures in Vedic history were warriors and kings who were also *yogis* and spiritual adepts. The inner requirements that are necessary for a person to master the disciplines of Yoga are very similar to those needed by a person to be a successful warrior. It is for this reason that many important *yogis* and sages in the Vedic tradition were former warriors who practiced spirituality with the discipline, focus, strength, courage and fortitude learned in their former careers as warriors. Not only does the Vedic tradition not encourage us to be in any way passive or weak, but in actuality, our tradition teaches us to be strong and assertive in the name of good and justice. Sanatana Dharma is not a path for sheep. Sanatana Dharma is a path of lions!

6) "Sanatana Dharma retards economic and social progress."

The very opposite of this stereotype is actually the truth. Sanatana Dharma is a path that stresses excellence in all areas of human concern. This dedication to excellence includes achieving greatness in both the spiritual and material realms. Sanatana Dharma teaches us that there is no necessary conflict between being both materially prosperous, while at the same time living the spiritually dedicated lifestyle expected of a devotee of God.

As a result of this positive reconciliation of the spiritual and material, Vedic nations, cultures and civilizations throughout world history have actually represented some of the most successful, technologically advanced and prosperous societies ever recorded. It is quite possible to have God in the center of our life, while simultaneously living a life of prosperity, abundance and success.

7) "Vedic culture is sexist or misogynistic."

This is one of the most malicious lies about the Vedic tradition in recent decades. The very opposite of this falsehood is the case. As has been exhaustively documented in the book *The Shakti Principle: Encountering the Feminine Power of God*,[11] Sanatana Dharma has always been one of the most empowering religions on earth for women.

It is in Sanatana Dharma, for example, that the sacred feminine aspect of God is fully understood and celebrated. Indeed, in Sanatana Dharma, God is referred to as Sriman Narayana. The term "Sriman" designates the feminine aspect of God, while the word "Narayana" describes the more masculine aspect of the same Absolute.

---

[11] This important book is available at Dharmacentral.com.

More, Sanatana Dharma encourages women to embrace leadership positions in every single echelon of our institutional hierarchy. Unlike the Abrahamic religions, in which it has only been in the 20th century that women have been allowed to serve in the clergy orders of some Abrahamic denominations, there have been many women priests, *yogis* (*yoginis*), *gurus* and *rishis* (seer-sages) throughout the history of Sanatana Dharma. Both women as an entire gender, as well as the metaphysical principle of feminine nature (*shakti*), are fully respected, honored and liberated in the Vedic tradition.

Chapter 8:

Vedic Contributions to the World

Seen within the historical context of the current era, which is known in the Vedic literature as the Kali Yuga (the last approximately 5100 years), Sanatana Dharma has been the origin of most of the important cultural, spiritual and civilizational foundations of the world. Even in examining only the era of modernity (the last roughly 250 years), the contributions of Sanatana Dharma to modern Western civilization have been immense. I will now list only a tiny portion of those contributions to our world.

Vegetarianism: Since the beginning of time, vegetarianism (not eating meat, fish or eggs) has been recognized by the tradition of Sanatana Dharma as the most natural and appropriate diet for making spiritual progress. While vegetarianism was also greatly appreciated by many European spiritual thinkers previous to the ascendency of Christianity, this rational dietary system was abandoned for many centuries in the West until Vedic spirituality – along with its vegetarian lifestyle - was reintroduced to Western shores in the 19th Century.

The Dharmic diet of lacto-vegetarianism (a diet free of meat, fish and eggs...but in which the consuming of such milk products as milk, cheese, yogurt and ghee is both acceptable and encouraged) has now been embraced by multiple tens of millions in America and Europe, and has been shown by a wide spectrum of the medical community to be one of the healthiest and most nutritious diets in the world. Indeed, the entire vegetarian and animal rights movement of the modern Western world owes its origins directly to the tradition of Sanatana Dharma, which was encouraging both vegetarianism and respect toward animals since the very beginning of time.

Natural Medicine: Natural and herbal medicine has its earliest known origins in the ancient Vedic scriptures. In these scriptures, natural medicine is known specifically as the system of Ayurveda, which is translated as "the Knowledge of Life". Included in the ancient system of Ayurveda are such practices as massage therapy, pranic healing, surgery, psychiatry, the balancing of the body's humours (*doshas*) and the use of medicinal plants, herbs, oils and tinctures to heal both body and mind. Ayurveda was the origin of such later medical developments as traditional Chinese medicine, ancient Greco-Roman medicine, and of the modern revival of natural and herbal medicine that has become so prevalent in the Western world today.

The traditional Dharmic medical system of Ayurveda is now being studied in many of the top medical colleges in the world as a safe, natural and highly effective sister-modality to the contemporary allopathic medicinal system. Its reemergence in the West has also led to the growth of the general field of natural medicine in the last 150 years that is now accepted and relied upon by the majority of people in all Western nations.[12] The origin of the modern trend of natural medicine is found rooted in the ancient tradition of Sanatana Dharma.

Yoga: It has always been understood in the tradition of Sanatana Dharma that authentic spirituality consists not only of philosophy and belief. It also consists of a systematic and revealed discipline of daily practice that is meant to progressively transform the spiritual practitioner toward achieving the highest goal of spirituality: existential liberation (*moksha*). We know by becoming. We become by doing. We do by the power of will. Such a systematic practice is known as *sadhana*. The *sadhana*, or system of spiritual practice, par excellence is known as Yoga.

---

[12] For further information on the ancient Vedic system of healing known as Ayurveda, visit Suryavedahealing.com.

was it here before?

With the historical ascendency of Abrahamism (beginning approximately 2000 BC), the sacred practices of Yoga, the Dharmic path of self-realization and God-consciousness, had slowly become lost outside much of South Asia and South-East Asia for many centuries. However, Yoga is once again being practiced by hundreds of millions of people throughout the entirely of the world – both East and West - for optimal health, stress-reduction, clarity of mind, as well as to experience the direct reality of their true spiritual selves. In America alone, over 20 million people practice Yoga on a regular basis.

The reason why so many millions of intelligent, educated, health-conscious, and spiritually-inclined people practice the Vedic discipline of Yoga is very simple: They have seen that it works. The Vedic path of Yoga provides its followers with peace of mind, mental clarity, calm, reduction of stress, and overall health like no other spiritual practice on earth. More, when they are practicing Yoga, they are practicing

Sanatana Dharma. Yoga is synonymous with, and non-separable from, the spiritual tradition of Sanatana Dharma.

Martial Arts: It is the unfortunate result of less than honest Hollywood marketing that has led to so many people to often mistakenly identify the origins of martial arts with the nations of East Asia (especially China and Japan). In actuality, most effective and stylized forms of martial arts originated within the creative incubator of Vedic culture many thousands of years before finally reaching China and the far East.

Such ancient and highly effective Vedic martial arts as *dhanur-veda* (Art of Archery), *shastra-vidya* (Art of Weaponry) and *svaraksha-kala* (Art of Self-Defense) form the foundation of all later forms of martial arts. Indeed, for those who understand the Vedic tradition in its authentic and scripturally-based form, it is understood that Sanatana Dharma is, above all, a warrior tradition. This being the case, it is not surprising to learn that martial arts were originally brought to their perfection in the Vedic tradition.

Respect for Nature: As we have already discussed, the very term "Sanatana Dharma" itself means the Eternal Natural Way. Sanatana Dharma is a path that is dedicated to understanding, respecting, as well as incorporating into our lives and into all culture and political governance, the eternal and unalterable ways of the natural order. Sanatana Dharma is the silent voice of nature translated to human understanding.

Followers of Dharma see the natural environment, not merely as a territory consisting of dead resources, but as a beautiful and balanced realm that is alive with meaning and personality. Loving nature and protecting the natural environment has been synonymous with the Dharma lifestyle since the very beginning of time.

With the ascendency of the Abrahamic religions (Judaism, mainstream Christianity and Islam) and materialism in the West, respect and love for nature had declined dramatically in the last 2000 years. It has only been in recent decades, in fact, that the Dharmic principles of environmental conservation and reverence for nature began to be reintroduced into the West in the form of the modern environmental and back to the land movements. Though known to few, many of the philosophical principles of the modern environmental sustainability movement owe their origins directly to the philosophical world-view of Sanatana Dharma.

Religious Tolerance: The history of religion in the last 2000 years has displayed many instances of destructive religious intolerance, persecution and wars based upon differences of religion. This has not been a general, religion-wide experience, however, but has been a negative behavioral phenomenon that has been conducted exclusively by the Abrahamic religions. Only the Abrahamic religions of Judaism, mainstream Christianity and Islam have been guilty of waging wars upon others based solely upon the need to convert their enemies to their religion.[13]

Dharma, on the other hand, teaches us to be reasonably tolerant and understanding of the fact that there will be differences of opinion and practice within the realm of religion. Dharma does not believe in persecuting others due to religious differences, or in an attempt to forcibly convert others to our way of practicing religion. As a result, throughout the history of the world, there have never been any "holy wars" of imperialistic religious conquest ever conducted in the name of Dharma.

[handwritten margin note: What about between Islam + Hinduism in India?]

While Sanatana Dharma clearly recognizes that religions are not all the same, and that there are some very real and insurmountable philosophical and

---

[13] Arguably, the Abrahamic-inspired ideology of Marxism has also been guilty of terrorizing "non-believers" in their pursuit of world dominance. In the case of Marxism, Socialism and Communism, the term "holy war" has been substituted by the term "revolution".

theological differences between many individual religious traditions, we believe in addressing these differences through peaceful dialogue and rational debate. We do not believe in responding to such differences of theological opinion with harsh arguments, hatred or violence.

This rational sense of religious tolerance that Sanatana Dharma practices began influencing the West in many profound ways, beginning especially in the 19th Century with the arrival of Swami Vivekananda and his famous talk at the Parliament of World Religions that took place in Chicago in 1893. Since that very event till today, there have been a multitude of interfaith conferences, meetings and organizing efforts, all dedicated to the attempt to reconcile religious differences through dialogue instead of violence. Such interfaith activities have all been conducted in instinctive imitation of the traditional Vedic way of dealing with religious differences of opinions – through respectful discussion, rather than fanatical diatribe and violence.

Freedom of Thought: Unlike many post-Vedic ideologies, Sanatana Dharma has always fostered a respect for freedom of honestly-held thought and expression. It is for this reason that, even though Sanatana Dharma is a unitary and eternal world-view, there have been a variety of expressions of Dharma over the last several millennia of the Kali Yuga (the current era).

Sanatana Dharma understands that part of the wonder of the human species is that we are all in different stages of advancement upon the path to Truth. Some individual persons are only beginning their path of spiritual exploration; some are very advanced in their understanding; and many are placed somewhere in the middle of their progress. As a result of this wide range of individual progress, and in reflection of these differences in evolvement, not everyone will necessarily share the exact same understanding of Truth, or even have the same motivation for why they are engaging in spiritual pursuit. Thus, we are to allow people to express themselves in accordance with where they currently find themselves in their progress of spiritual development.

In the Abrahamic world, the idea of such an allowance of freedom of honestly-held thought and opinion was often met with tremendous skepticism and even persecution. Indeed, the history of much of the last 2000 years in the Abrahamic world has been one of censorship, Inquisitions, jihads, genocides and fatwas against those ideas that the Abrahamic and materialist overlords deemed to be too "dangerous" to their control and power. In the last several centuries, however, the ancient principle of freedom of thought that was always central to Vedic culture has now been slowly reintroduced to the Western world.

The Rule of Law: Many of us take the existence of the rule of law for granted today. The fact of the matter, though, is that various eras throughout the history of the human species within the last 5100 years have resembled a widely swinging pendulum between some societies that respected the rule of law, and some societies in which codified law was all but non-existent. Whenever there have been advanced civilizations that did respect the rule of law, almost all of these societies recognized that equitable and just systems of legislation and jurisprudence can only have legitimacy when they are based upon the principles of Natural Law.

Though these law-respecting societies may not necessarily have equated the concept of Natural Law with the specific Sanskrit term "Dharma", Natural Law is ultimately synonymous with the concept of Dharma nonetheless. The origin of the very concept of Rule of Law is itself predicated upon the existence of Dharma, laws of the universe that are eternal, unalterable and universally applicable. If we have any faith that we can seek justice in a court of law today, we owe such faith to the foundation of Dharma upon which all just law is either directly or indirectly predicated.

The Shakti Principle: The nature and role of the feminine principle has a special place of honor in Vedic metaphysics. Unlike the Abrahamic religions, for whom their god is an unmistakably male figure, Sanatana Dharma recognizes that both the masculine and the feminine metaphysical principles have their own important roles in understanding the essence of God.

The Shakti Principle is a central concept in Sanatana Dharma. This principle teaches us that God has both a feminine and a masculine side. In a somewhat similar way in which the god of mainstream Christianity is seen as a trinity, the Supreme God is understood in Sanatana Dharma to be a dual being consisting of God/Goddess. The names of the feminine and masculine aspects of God are, respectively, Lakshmi and Narayana, or more formally: Sriman Narayana. Sriman Narayana is the highest name for God in the Vedic tradition.

More, the feminine aspect of God is seen as manifest in every earthly woman as well. It is for this reason that, thousands of years before the modern, Marxist-inspired movement known as "feminism" even exited as an idea, women have held a place of respect, honor and leadership in Vedic society. Unlike the Abrahamic religions, women have always been encouraged to be leaders, sages, saints and great *gurus* in Sanatana Dharma. This Vedic respect for the inherent dignity of woman has now finally begun to influence and transform how Western religions view the divine feminine. The spirituality of the divine feminine has its origins in Sanatana Dharma.[14]

European Pre-Christian Spiritual Revival: Having suffered from the dark and oppressive dogmas of Abrahamism for many centuries, Europe began to reembrace its illustrious pre-Christian spiritual and cultural heritage during the Renaissance Era. From

---

[14] Read my book, *The Shakti Principle*, for much more information about this important aspect of Sanatana Dharma. Available at Dharmacentral.com.

that historical time period until the present day, many millions of Europeans and Americans have rejected Biblical religion altogether in favor of the more life-affirming religions of ancient Europe that were practiced previous to the forced imposition of Christianity upon the traditional peoples of Europe.

The ancient religions of Europe were the European equivalent of Sanatana Dharma. Ancient European religions and Sanatana Dharma were, and are, sister religions. Some of these pre-Christian European religions include Greco-Roman, Asatru (Nordic), Celtic and Slavic. Due to the fact that much of the original teachings and practices of these pre-Christian European religions have been irretrievably lost, almost all of the reconstruction efforts to revive these ancient European religions have relied very heavily upon borrowing directly from the teachings and practices of Sanatana Dharma. Thus, the modern reconstruction of pre-Christian European religions would not have been possible without the leaders of this revival turning to their elder sister: Sanatana

Dharma.

Likewise, the pre-Islamic religions of the Arab world and Iran are in the process of being reconstructed with the help of the Vedic tradition. As followers of Sanatana Dharma, it is our joyful honor to assist in the revival of all pre-Abrahamic religions. Such religions are our sister Dharmic traditions, and we look forward to seeing them fully restored and practiced again in the future.

Famous Followers of Sanatana Dharma: Dharmic ideas, philosophy, spirituality, and art have influenced more people throughout world history than any other religion on earth. Among the thought leaders and artists in the West who have been highly influenced by the teachings of Sanatana Dharma are: Arthur Schopenhauer, Herman Melville, Ralph Waldo Emerson, Henry David Thoreau, Walt Whitman, Mark Twain, Romain Rolland, Albert Einstein, Aldous Huxley, J. Robert Oppenheimer, Christopher Isherwood, J.D. Salinger, Arlo Guthrie, George

Harrison, Chrissie Hynde, movie director David Lynch, and actors Russell Brand, Julia Roberts and Heather Graham, among the many thousands of other well-known writers, intellectuals, scientists, celebrities, musicians and artists who have incorporated aspects of Sanatana Dharma into their lives. Tom Brady, quarterback for the New England Patriots football team, keeps a four inch statue of Ganesha in his locker. Even today, tens of thousands of famous celebrities, scientists and scholars in both Europe and America find spiritual solace and intellectual assurance in the amazing teachings of Dharma.

Sanatana Dharma is a religious path that is open to all sincere seekers, regardless of whether they are educated or not, famous or not, or whether they are rich or poor. In the next chapter, we will take a look at the most important and dynamic Vedic movement in the world today: the International Sanatana Dharma Society. If you would like to begin practicing Sanatana Dharma in a way that is guaranteed to be rooted in the authenticity of the Vedic scriptures, then I would suggest that you take full advantage of the many educational, community and *sadhana* opportunities offered by the ISDS by becoming a member today.

Chapter 9:
International Sanatana Dharma Society

The International Sanatana Dharma Society (ISDS) is a global spiritual movement dedicated to practicing and teaching the ancient Vedic religious tradition in its fully authentic and unaltered form. Our goal in spiritual practice is to accept no watering-down or compromises to the time-honored integrity of the Vedic philosophy and lifestyle. The only way to practice and truly benefit from Dharma spirituality is to practice Dharma on its own sacred terms, and not merely as a further extension of our ego (*ahamkara*).

Our religion is known in the Sanskrit language as Sanatana Dharma, or the Eternal Natural Way. We thus call ourselves "Dharmis", or followers of Dharma. Members of the ISDS follow Sanatana Dharma exclusively as their chosen religious path. We do not mix and match pure Vedic spirituality with any other religious traditions, modern "new age" innovations, or pop spirituality. We exclusively identify with, and practice, Sanatana Dharma as our path to Self-realization and God-consciousness.

We know truth by means of a) the instructing words and guidance of the enlightened *guru* (*guru-vani*), b) the guidance of the revealed Vedic scriptures (*Shastra-pramana*), and c) the use of our own reasoning faculties (*vichara*), philosophical discernment (*viveka*) and personal experience (*anubhava*). Sanatana Dharma is not a religion of blind faith, fanaticism, or wishful thinking. It is a religion of acquired spiritual / philosophical wisdom, coupled with direct personal experience of the transformative presence of God.

The teachings and practices of the ISDS are based directly upon the Vedic scriptures. Our scriptures consist of the entire *shruti* and *smriti* cannons of the Vedic literature, but with special emphasis on the teachings of the *Bhagavad Gita, Upanishads, Bhagavata Purana, Vishnu Purana, Yoga Sutras, Brahma Sutras* and *Narada Bhakti Sutras.*

Aum Tad Vishnu Paramam Padam

"The abode of Vishnu is the highest state of existence." (*Rig Veda*, 1:22:20)

Members of the ISDS recognize the Vedic scriptures' clear declaration that Sriman Narayana (also known as Vishnu) represents the supreme form of Godhead (Brahman), and we express special devotion to the avatara of Sriman Narayana for this age: Bhagavan Sri Krishna and His divine consort (*divya-shakti*) Srimati Radharani. Sri Krishna was on the earth over 5100 years ago, and is the speaker of the famous *Bhagavad Gita*, the most important scripture for our current age. The meaning of life is to revive our innate devotional consciousness (*bhakti*) toward the Supreme Godhead, and to reunite ourselves with Sriman Narayana in eternal loving union.

Our spiritual practice (*sadhana*) consists of the full classical Yoga system (*ashtanga*) permeated throughout with a consciousness of *bhakti* (devotion). *Bhakti*, or devotional consciousness, is understood to be both the highest means of liberation, as well as the ultimate goal of spiritual life and culture. Thus, *bhakti* is not merely the most effective means (*upaya*) for spiritual liberation; it is also the ultimate goal (*paramartha*) of life. Members of the ISDS all strive to achieve Self-realization (*atma-jnana*), leading finally to God-consciousness (*brahma-vidya*).

Our primary form of meditation is mantra meditation upon the divine sound vibration:

Aum Namo Narayanaya

Distinctly Authentic Approach to Vedic Spirituality

There are several features that make the International Sanatana Dharma Society (ISDS) fundamentally distinctive when compared to any other Hindu /

Dharma / Yoga movement on earth today.

1) Guru Principle: We recognize that it is only under the expert guidance and grace of an authentic *guru* that we can traverse the path to liberation safely and effectively. We are guided, both as individual disciples and as a movement, by a living and extremely qualified representative of the Vedic ideal in the form of our enlightened spiritual teacher.

2) Scripturally-Based: We scrupulously base everything the ISDS does and teaches upon a clear understanding of the Vedic scriptures. Our approach to philosophy, spiritual practice, meditation and lifestyle are all rooted directly in the teachings of the scriptures. Indeed, in-depth and guided study of the Vedic scriptures is one of the most important ongoing practices that our members engage in.

3) Academic Excellence: Our members strongly strive to couple their meditative spiritual practice with a very scholarly and philosophical grasp of the philosophy, theology, culture, history and application of Sanatana Dharma. Mystical attainment can never be used as an excuse for intellectual lethargy on the part of the spiritual practitioner. Success on the spiritual path is only possible with the integrative partnership of both subjective spiritual experience (*anubhava*) coupled with wisdom and understanding (*buddhi*).

4) Quality over Quantity: In our philosophy and practices (both personal and as an organizational structure), the ISDS always emphasizes the spiritual quality of our activities over mere quantity. Thus, rather than artificially focusing on only having a large mass following, we instead strive to have a smaller membership of truly exceptional and sincere spiritual practitioners. Consequently, we have sometimes been called somewhat elitist or exclusive in whom we accept as members and formal students. We're fine with that!

Our goal is to serve those who are sincerely ready for the real thing: an authentic path the goal of which is having a direct experience of truth. We also seek to create the Dharma leaders and teachers of the future who will carry on the traditions of the most ancient spiritual path on earth. The ISDS represents nothing less than the cutting-edge Vedic vanguard. The ISDS is thus not for everyone. But if you are willing to learn and practice authentic Vedic spirituality in a mood of humility and sincerity, and to experience growth in your spiritual life in a manner that is truly meaningful, then you are very welcome to join.

5) Vedic Authenticity: We are radical traditionalists in our approach to the Vedic way. We seek to practice Dharma in as traditional, authentic, orthodox and uncompromisingly real a manner as is possible in the modern era. There is nothing new, "New Age", or concocted in how we teach or practice the Vedic way. Moreover, we do not "mix and blend" our practice or understanding of Sanatana Dharma with those of other, non-Vedic paths. If you are interested in the ISDS, and being involved in our movement, please do so knowing that what you will be taught and will be following is nothing less than the authentic and ancient religion of Sanatana Dharma - the Eternal Natural Way.

6) Comprehensiveness: As students of the Vedic way, we understand that Sanatana Dharma is so much more than merely a religious tradition. Rather, the world-view, arts and sciences of Vedic culture are meant to very naturally extend into every field of human concern. This includes not only the spiritual, but also the social, political, economic, scientific, medical, artistic, musical, culinary, martial, cultural, civilizational and philosophical realms of human endeavor. The ISDS seeks to not only help our members in their own individual spiritual progress, but to also extend the truths of Dharma over the entire sphere of human endeavor. Our goal is to change all of society on the most fundamental of levels, and to thus affect the re-spiritualization of global civilization.

7) Effective Sadhana: The powerful spiritual disciplines that the ISDS teaches its members are highly effective, authorized and scripturally-based, with an emphasis on Yoga, *mantra*, *puja*, and meditation as revealed in the *Upanishads*. Our *sadhana* techniques are known to provide practitioners with an immediate experience of spiritual bliss and realization. At the same time, however, it is understood that *sadhana* is a long-term commitment that will eventually deepen a person's spiritual realization over time. *Sadhana* is not merely some magical amusement. It is a commitment.

8) Highest Ethical Standards: Many in the West have all too often found themselves exploited by unethical "spiritual teachers" who falsely claimed to be representing the pure Yoga and Dharma tradition, but who only turned out to be amoral abusers of their innocent followers. The ISDS is unyielding in its commitment to upholding and educating all its members in the very highest ethical standards that form the core behavioral expectations of Vedic culture.

Our strict code of ethics includes adherence to the Yamas and Niyamas of Yoga philosophy. Both the initiated students and the leaders of the ISDS are expected, without exception, to strictly observe the following ethical standards: a) no intoxicants (including alcohol, cigarettes, marijuana, hashish, ayahuasca, etc.), b) strict lacto-vegetarianism (no meat, fish or eggs), c) no illicit or exploitative sexual behavior (sexuality should be confined exclusively to the institution of monogamous marriage between one man and one woman). It is only in demanding the very highest ethical standards of its leaders that the dignity of Sanatana Dharma can be upheld.

Becoming a Member of the ISDS

We recognize that membership in the ISDS is not for everyone. Our students are dedicated to following a path that encourages them to look honestly within in a contemplative manner, to observing a spiritual discipline that leads to a gradual unfoldment of their true selves, and that results in Self-realization and God-consciousness.

If you are interested in joining the International Sanatana Dharma Society, we ask that you possess deep sincerity, humility, intellectual openness, and a strong desire to know the Divine. If you are attracted to a Vedic-based path that focuses on thorough authenticity, a conscientious philosophical approach, and a clear and effective means of knowing God's presence in your everyday life, please consider becoming an official member today.

The following are requirements for membership:

1. You must consider Sanatana Dharma to be your spiritual tradition.

2. All members are expected to donate monthly in accordance with their means.

Please choose a generous amount below, and start giving your tax-deductible monthly membership donation today!

Membership Tiers

1. <u>Basic Membership</u>: $120 minimum annual donation. ($10 per month)

2. <u>Family Membership</u>: $240 minimum annual donation. ($20 per month)

3. Supporting Member (Dharma Warrior): $600 minimum annual donation. ($50 per month)

4. Patron Member (Dharma Knight): $1200 minimum annual donation. ($100 per month)

5. Life Member (Dharma King/Queen): $5000 minimum one time donation.

For more information on how to become a member, please visit:

www.dharmacentral.com/membership.html

It is my sincere hope that this Introduction to Sanatana Dharma has provided you with an informative and inspiring overview of the religious tradition of Sanatana Dharma. I also hope that, if you have found the answers that you are looking for in this path, you will consider becoming a Dharmi today. If you desire further guidance in deepening your understanding and practice of the Vedic path, please contact the International Sanatana Dharma Society today.

Resources

Books by Sri Dharma Pravartaka Acharya

Sanatana Dharma: The Eternal Natural Way

The Sanatana Dharma Study Guide

The Dharma Manifesto

The Vedic Way of Knowing God

Living Dharma: The Teachings of Sri Dharma Pravartaka Acharya

Radical Universalism: Are All Religions the Same?

Taking Refuge in Dharma: The Initiation Guidebook

The Shakti Principle: Encountering the Feminine Power of God

Introduction to Sanatana Dharma

Principles of Leadership

Lord of the Rings, Dharma and Modernity

The Vedic Encyclopedia

Narada Bhakti Sutras: Translation and Commentary

Vedanta: The Culmination of Wisdom

The Dharma of Wellbeing

Jnana Yoga: The Art of Wisdom

The Dharma Dialogues

Isha Upanishad: Translation and Commentary

Books by A.C. Bhaktivedanta Swami Prabhupada

Bhagavad-Gita as It Is

Krsna: The Supreme Personality of Godhead

The Nectar of Devotion: The Complete Science of Bhakti Yoga

The Perfection of Yoga

Sri Isopanisad

Easy Journey to Other Planets

The Science of Self-Realization

Raja-vidya: The King of Knowledge

Dharma Websites

Dharmacentral.com

Dharmacivilization.com

Dharmanation.org

Youtube.com/DharmaNation

Bitchute.com/SanatanaDharma

Suryavedahealing.com

Facebook.com/pages/International-Sanatana-Dharma-Society/111383025561439

About the Author

Sri Dharma Pravartaka Acharya is universally acclaimed as one of the world's most respected and qualified Dharma teachers and Vedic spiritual leaders. Dr. Deepak Chopra has exclaimed in 2002: "You've done truly phenomenal work teaching the pure essence of Yoga". In a similar manner, Dr. David Frawley has said about Sri Acharyaji, "Sri Acharyaji represents the Sankalpa [the will] of the Hindu people and the cause of Sanatana Dharma. I urge all Hindus everywhere to give him your full support, assistance, and encouragement in his crucial work. He needs and deserves our help." Indeed, *Hinduism Today Magazine* has proclaimed him one of the top five scholars of Hinduism on earth.

Sri Acharyaji began his personal spiritual journey over 45 years ago at the tender age of ten when he read the *Bhagavad Gita* for the very first time. It was at the age of ten that he began his rigorous practice of Yoga, meditation, *pranayama* and many other ancient Vedic techniques of spiritual awakening. At approximately twelve years old, he took Yoga lessons from Sri Dharma Mittra and Sri Swami Bua in New York City. Only a few short years later, he took on the lifestyle of a fulltime Vedic monk, living a strict life of monastic vows and great austerity for close to eight years. This monastic training culminated in Sri Acharyaji being awarded the status of *brahmana* (Vedic priest) by his *guru*, B.R. Sridhara Swami, in 1986 at his *guru's ashrama* in India.

He coupled his decades of intense spiritual practice and study with advanced academic achievements, earning a B.A. in philosophy/theology from Loyola University Chicago, as well as an M.A. and Ph.D. in religious studies from the University of Wisconsin-Madison. His entire university career was funded by academic fellowships awarded to him as a result of his scholastic excellence and brilliance.

Explaining to his doctoral advisor in 1995 that *"I don't want to just study the history of religion...I want to make religious history"*, Sri Acharyaji eventually left academia to devote himself exclusively to spiritual teaching and to the preservation of the great tradition of Sanatana Dharma.

Sri Acharyaji occupies his full time teaching Dharma spirituality to diverse audiences. In addition to leading classes, *satsanghas*, seminars and lecturing on Sanatana Dharma widely, Sri Acharyaji is a renowned author of over ten authoritative books, as well as a personal spiritual guide (*guru*) to a rapidly increasing following of many thousands of enthusiastic students from both the Indian and the non-Indian communities.

Sri Acharyaji was the Resident Acharya (Spiritual Preceptor) of the Hindu Temple of Nebraska from 2007-2009, which represents the first time in American history that a Hindu temple has ever made such an esteemed appointment. Sri Acharyaji is considered by many contemporary *gurus* and leaders of the Vedic community to be the most cutting-edge, authentic and highly qualified Vedic *guru* in the world today.

Members of the ISDS acknowledge Sri Acharyaji as a truly enlightened sage, as a *Sad-guru* (true *guru*) capable of guiding his disciples to the deepest realization of wisdom and spiritual liberation, and all members strive to follow his spiritual teachings in our daily lives with sincerity, loyalty and fidelity.

For more information about the life and teachings of Sri Dharma Pravartaka Acharya, please visit his website: www.dharmacentral.com

Glossary

Abhaya:	Fearlessness.
Abhyasa:	Practice.
Acharya:	Spiritual Preceptor. Guru. Representative of a spiritual lineage.
Acharya-asana:	Seat of the Acharya.
Ahamkara:	The artificial and illusory sense of self, lit. "I-maker."
Aham Pratyaya:	I-Cognition. The healthy sense of "I" as distinct from others.
Ahimsa:	Non-violence, including vegetarianism.
Ananda:	Bliss, happiness, enjoyment.
Aparigraha:	Non-possession, one of the five yamas (abstinences) of ashtanga-yoga.
Artha:	Aim, purpose, goal, meaning.

Asana: The physical poses of the Yoga system.

Ashrama: A retreat, hermitage, or secluded place where the principles of yoga and meditation are practiced.

Asteya: Non-stealing, non-theft, one of the five yamas (abstinences) of ashtanga-yoga.

Atman: The true, eternal, essential self.

AUM: Divine sound representing the omni-presence of God. The primordial sound out of which all other sounds are born.

Avatara: A Divine descent of God into the earthly manifestation. Avataras of God come to earth to uphold Dharma and to battle adharma.

Avidya: Ignorance.

Bhagavad Gita: The Song of God. The

	primary scripture of Sanatana Dharma.
Bhakti:	Devotional consciousness.
Brahmachari:	Celibate student.
Brahmacharya:	Sexual restraint, one of the five yamas (abstinences) of ashtanga-yoga.
Buddha:	Awakened. The avatara of God seen as the founder of Buddhism.
Buddhi:	Wisdom Faculty, intellect, understanding.
Chaitanya:	Consciousness.
Chakra:	Wheel, circle. Symbol of Dharma. One of seven psychic energy centers in the subtle body.
Chit:	Knowledge.
Chitta:	Psyche. Mind-substance, reason, and intelligence.

Dana: Charity.

Darshana: View, perspective, observation, seeing. The philosophical systems of Sanatana Dharma are known as Darshanas. They all recognize the insights of the Vedas as their foundation. Darshana also means to view a sacred image or to have the audience of a sage.

Deva/Devi: Lesser gods/goddesses of Vedic spirituality. Similar to angels in the West.

Dharana: Concentration, the sixth of the eight limbs of Yoga.

Dharma: Natural Law/Way. Intrinsic principles of cosmic operation.

Dharmi: A follower of Sanatana Dharma.

Dhyana: Meditation, the seventh of the

	eight limbs of Yoga.
Diksha:	Spiritual initiation by a qualified guru.
Duhkha:	Dissatisfaction, pain, sorrow, frustration.
Drashtr:	The seer, experiencer, consciousness, atman.
Guna:	The three constituents of prime matter, which are: sattva (lightness, radiance or illumination), rajas (activity or passion), tamas: (darkness, ignorance or inertia).
Guru:	Teacher. Spiritual mentor and guide.
Ishvara:	Literally master, lord, or king. Another term for God. Narayana.
Ishvara-pranidhana:	Devotion to Ishvara, selfless action, one of the five niyamas (observances) of Yoga.

Japa:	Repetition of a mantra.
Japa-mala:	A sting of 108 beads used for mantra meditation.
Jaya:	Mastery, conquering, victory.
Jñana:	Wisdom, knowledge, understanding.
Kali-yuga:	The present historical cyclic era. The Age of Conflict.
Karma:	"Action". The principle that for every action, there is a reaction.
Karuna:	Compassion toward all sentient beings.
Krishna:	The last incarnation of God who appeared on earth over 5100 years ago. The speaker of the Bhagavad Gita. The primary form of God to be worshipped in this age.
Krodha:	Anger, wrath, passion.

Maha Jagad Guru:	Great World Teacher.
Mantra:	A Divine, liberating sound vibration.
Mantra-dhyana:	Mantra meditation.
Maya:	Illusion.
Moksha:	Liberation, spiritual freedom.
Murti:	Sacred image placed on altars and used in worshipful meditation.
Namaste:	"I offer my respects to you". A respectful greeting.
Narayana:	One of the primary names of God. The "Sustainer of All Beings".
Narayana-mantra:	Aum Namo Narayanaya. "I offer my respects to that Absolute Who is the sustainer of all beings".
Niyama:	Observances. One of the eight limbs of Yoga. The niyamas

are shauca (purity), santosha (contentment), tapas (austerity), svadhyaya (self-study) and Ishvara-pranidhana (devotion to Ishvara or God).

Patañjali: The author of the Yoga Sutras believed to have lived around 300 B.C.

Prakriti: Material nature. Prime matter. The power of creativity.

Prana: Life energy, life force, or life current. These finer-than-atomic energies have inherent intelligence, as opposed to atoms and electrons, which are considered to be blind forces. The Chinese call this life force chi.

Pranayama: Yoga breathing exercises. Pranayama is one of the eight limbs of Yoga.

Pratyahara:	Withdrawing the senses in order to still the mind in meditation. One of the eight limbs of Yoga.
Prasada:	"Grace". Food or other objects offered to God and thus sanctified.
Prema:	Divine love.
Puja:	Worship ceremony.
Rishi:	Seer, sage, perfected yogi, revealer of sacred texts.
Sadhana:	Spiritual practice or discipline.
Sadhaka:	One who performs sadhana.
Samadhi:	Absorption of our consciousness in God, unitive awareness, eighth limb of Yoga.
Samsara:	The wheel of material existence. The cycle of birth and death.

Sanatana Dharma: The Eternal Natural Way. The true name of the spiritual tradition commonly mislabeled "Hinduism".

Santosha: Contentment. One of the niyamas.

Sat-sangha: True/Good association.

Sattva: Illumination, lightness, one of the three gunas.

Satya: Truthfulness, one of the five yamas (abstinences) of Yoga.

Shanti: Peace.

Shastra: Scripture.

Shauca: Purity, one of the five niyamas (observances) of Yoga.

Sriman-Narayana: The highest name of God in Sanatana Dharma. It denotes both the male and female aspects of God together, Mother-Father God in the form of Sri Lakshmi and Narayana.

Sutra: Lit. "thread"; a brief statement or aphorism often used to convey Dharma philosophy in brevity of form.

Svadhyaya: Self-study, one of the five niyamas (observances) of Yoga.

Tamas: Heaviness, darkness, inertia. One of the three gunas.

Tapas: Austerity, asceticism, challenging oneself. One of the five niyamas of Yoga.

Tulasi: A plant that is very dear to Lord Narayana, and thus sacred.

Upanishads: Ancient Vedic philosophical scriptures. There are 108 Upanishads in total.

Veda(s): "Knowledge". The sacred

scriptures (shastras) of Sanatana Dharma.

Vidya:	Wisdom, science, knowledge.
Viveka:	Discrimination, discernment.
Vairagya:	Detachment.
Vedanta:	Philosophical school propounded by Badarayana Vyasa. It contains the teachings of the Upanishads and investigates the nature and relationship of the three Reals (Tri-tattva): the Absolute (Brahman), Materiality (Jagat), and the finite self (Atman).
Yama:	Restraint. One of the eight limbs of Yoga.
Yamas & Niyamas:	The ten ethical principles of Dharma.
Yoga:	"Union". The systematic path, discipline, and philosophy for God-realization.

For authoritative and much more in-depth explanations of these, and many hundreds more, Sanskrit terms, refer to my book *The Vedic Encyclopedia.*

Printed in Great Britain
by Amazon

25380673R00096